Living with Lovejoy

Written by
Kate Morrow

Illustrated by
Rashida Mohamed Juma

Living with Lovejoy
Copyright © Never Forget Publishing 2015

ISBN # 978-0-9962576-7-1

Special thanks to Holly Scholl, Brittney Cox, and Chelsea Mentado, student designers at Augustana College.

A BOOK
Human Rights Series

History comes alive with true stories written by children for children

NEVER FORGET PUBLISHING

A BOOK by ME is dedicated to the Quad Cities' Three Esthers

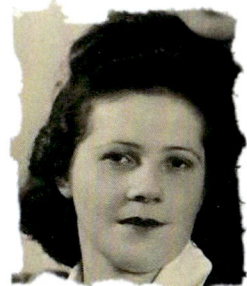  

Esther Avruch   **Esther Katz**   **Esther Schiff**

Also, lovingly dedicated to Ida Kramer, Holocaust Historian, & Edith Levy, Jewish Holocaust Survivor & Author

MISSION STATEMENT:
A BOOK by ME® seeks to preserve the history of the Holocaust and other human rights issues. Our desire is to preserve the stories for the next generation so lessons of tolerance, empathy, hope and respect are not lost.

To deny people their human rights is to challenge their very humanity.

Nelson Mandela

Dear Reader,

I've had the honor of working at the Lovejoy Homestead by giving tours to those interested. The home of the Denham and Lovejoy family is located on the eastern edge of Princeton, Illinois. This is my hometown and I'm very proud of our rich heritage.

Reverend Lovejoy is our most famous resident. He lived in Princeton from 1838 until his death in 1864. Our hero was a congressional leader and a founder of the national Republican Party. He is most well known because his home was an important stop for runaway slaves in the Underground Railroad. Here are some interesting facts about Owen Lovejoy:

Name:	Owen Lovejoy
Born:	Albion, Maine in 1811
Story:	1836 - Owen moved to Alton, Illinois (across the Mississippi River from Missouri, a slave state) to be with his older brother, Elijah, and study for the ministry. Elijah was the editor of an anti-slavery newspaper and was eventually murdered by an angry mob of pro-slavery citizens. After his death, Owen devoted the rest of his life to the abolitionist cause.

Owen Lovejoy

1838 - Owen came to Princeton, a village of about 200 people, to be the minister of the Hampshire Colony Congregational Church. He held that position for seventeen years, preaching his strong views against slavery.

Lovejoy was friends with President Abraham Lincoln and was a guest at the historical signing of the Emancipation Proclamation. I hope you enjoy this book and learning about this brave man named Owen Lovejoy.

Sincerely,
Kate Morrow
Princeton, Illinois

Reverend Owen Lovejoy was an abolitionist. He was a minister and a true "Renaissance Man." He was a station master on the Underground Railroad, a Congressman, a colonel in the Civil War, a husband, and a father. He dedicated his life to a cause he truly believed in, and he sacrificed many valuable things to pursue his work.

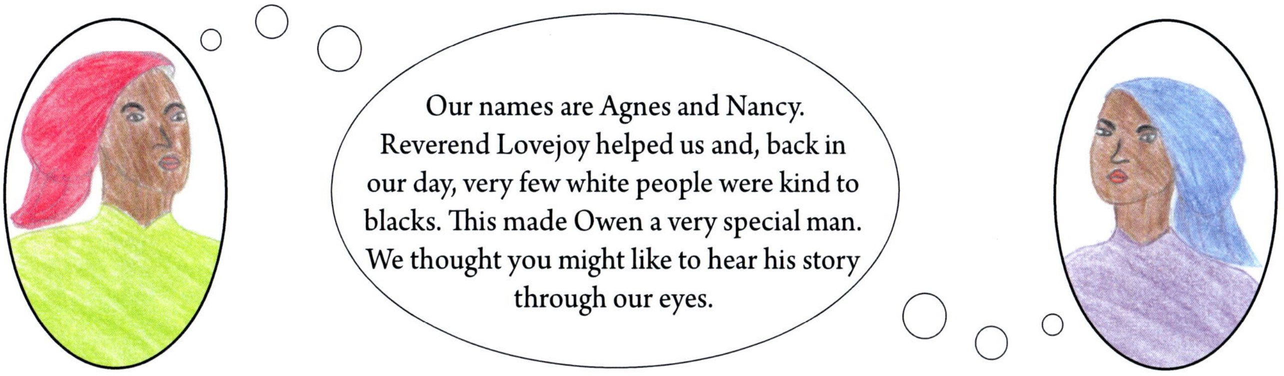

Our names are Agnes and Nancy. Reverend Lovejoy helped us and, back in our day, very few white people were kind to blacks. This made Owen a very special man. We thought you might like to hear his story through our eyes.

Owen was born in 1811 in Maine. He grew up and went to school there, but eventually moved to Illinois to join his brother, Elijah, in Alton. Elijah published an abolitionist newspaper there, despite the local opposition to slavery. In 1837, Elijah was assassinated by a mob attacking his printing press, and Owen vowed to carry on Elijah's dedication to abolition for the rest of his life.

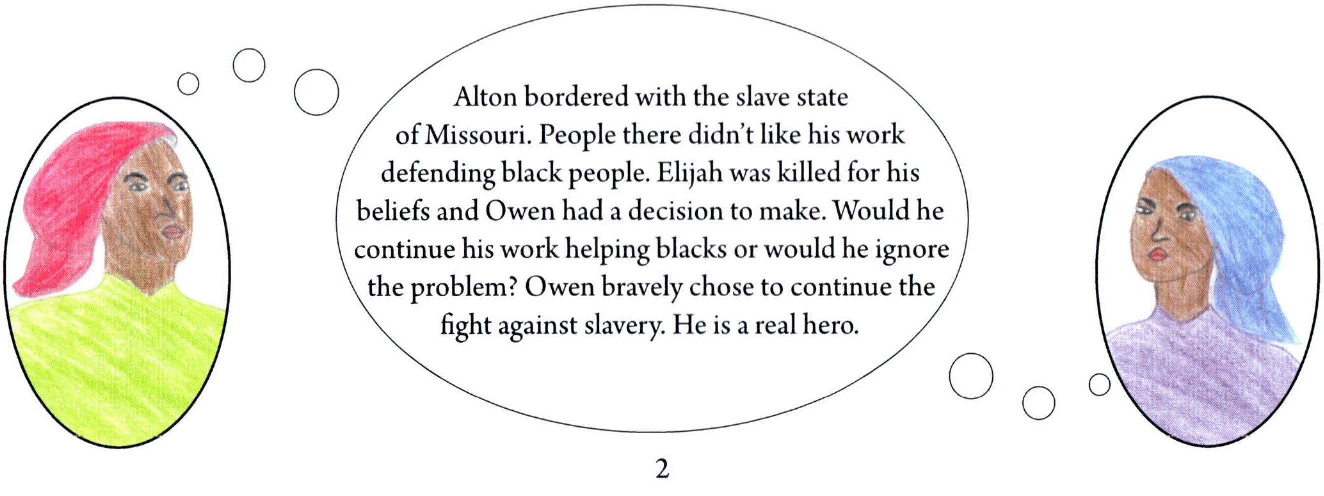

Alton bordered with the slave state of Missouri. People there didn't like his work defending black people. Elijah was killed for his beliefs and Owen had a decision to make. Would he continue his work helping blacks or would he ignore the problem? Owen bravely chose to continue the fight against slavery. He is a real hero.

Owen moved to Princeton in 1838 to take a job as a minister in the Hampshire Colony Congregational Church. Originally, Owen wanted to work at an Episcopal church; however, all Episcopal churches made their priests sign a legal document promising never to preach abolition in the church. Because Owen's views against slavery were so strong, he could never agree to their rules. Instead, Owen came to Princeton, a small village of about 200 people, where he made a salary of $600 a year. While living in Princeton, Owen needed a place to live. He found a family to provide room and board just outside of town. The family consisted of Mr. Butler Denham, his wife Eunice, and their three daughters.

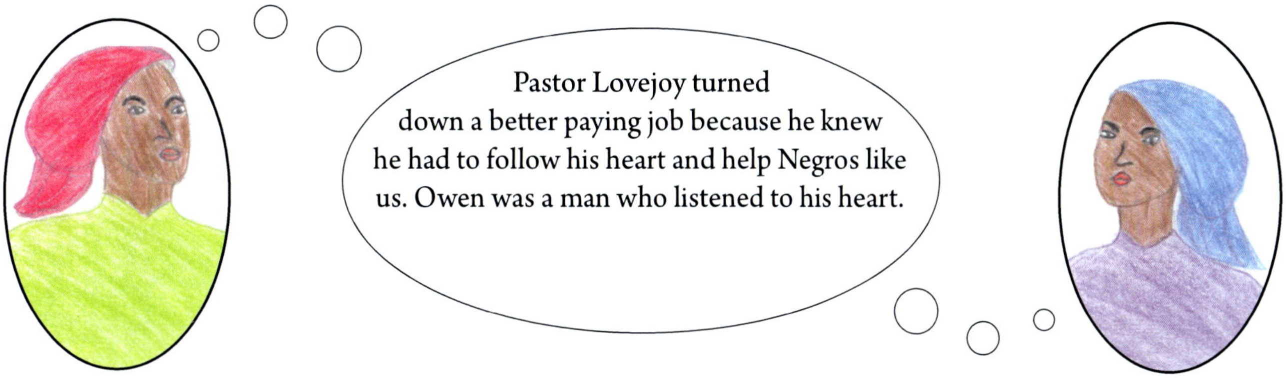

Pastor Lovejoy turned down a better paying job because he knew he had to follow his heart and help Negros like us. Owen was a man who listened to his heart.

Owen lived a good life in Princeton. The Denham's were also abolitionists, and Owen got along well with the whole family. He read Bible verses to them after dinner, and they talked of politics and slavery. Just three years after Owen moved in with them, Mr. Denham died suddenly, leaving behind a farm and a family.

After a proper period of mourning, Eunice remarried. Her new husband was a very close friend, Owen Lovejoy. They were married in 1843, and they continued working on the farm, fighting for abolition, and raising children—eventually having six more!

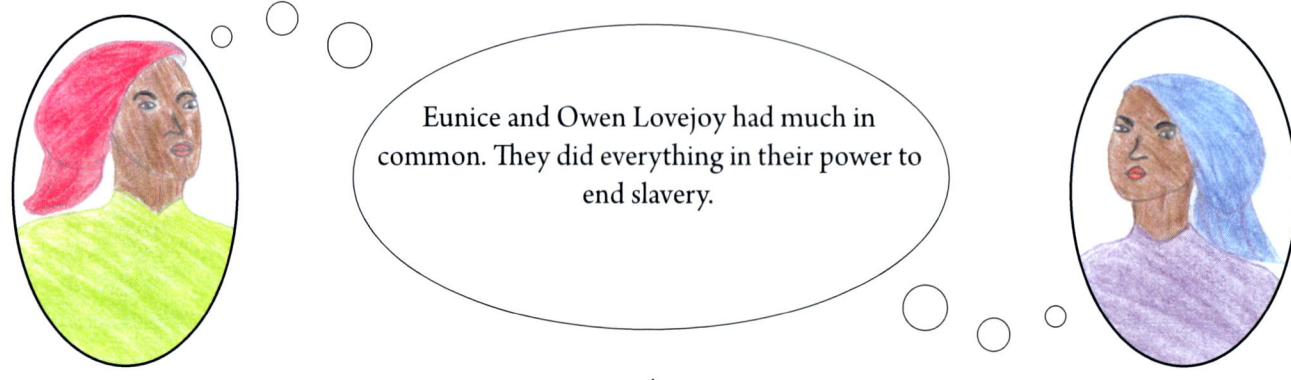

Eunice and Owen Lovejoy had much in common. They did everything in their power to end slavery.

Owen was so passionate about his cause that he and Eunice hid escaping slaves in their own home as part of the Underground Railroad. The slaves would come from the South, up the Mississippi River, and then Northward on their way to Canada—and freedom. They walked for most of their journey, only occasionally hiding on a boat or in an abolitionist's carriage. Owen never denied his beliefs nor his actions. In fact, he openly declared that he had harbored slaves on their journey to freedom in a speech to Congress:

"*No human being, black or white, bond or free, native or foreign, ever came to my door and asked for food and shelter, who did not receive it. This I have done. This I mean to do as long as God lets me live. Proclaim it then upon the housetops. Write it on every leaf that trembles in the forest, make it blaze from the sun at high noon. Owen Lovejoy lives at Princeton, Illinois, three-quarters of a mile east of the village, and he aids every fugitive that comes to his door and asks it. Thou invisible demon of Slavery, does thou think to cross my humble threshold, and forbid me to give bread to the hungry and shelter to the houseless?*"

Sometimes it's hard to believe one man could be so brave. Very few people could do what Owen Lovejoy was able to do. You have to respect someone like him.

Owen helped a number of slaves over the years, and he even went to court for hiding fugitives. Owen was accused of helping two slaves, Agnes and Nancy. To avoid being convicted, Owen argued that they were living in Illinois, a free state; therefore, they were free people. He had done nothing wrong and broken no laws by helping these two women as they came through town.

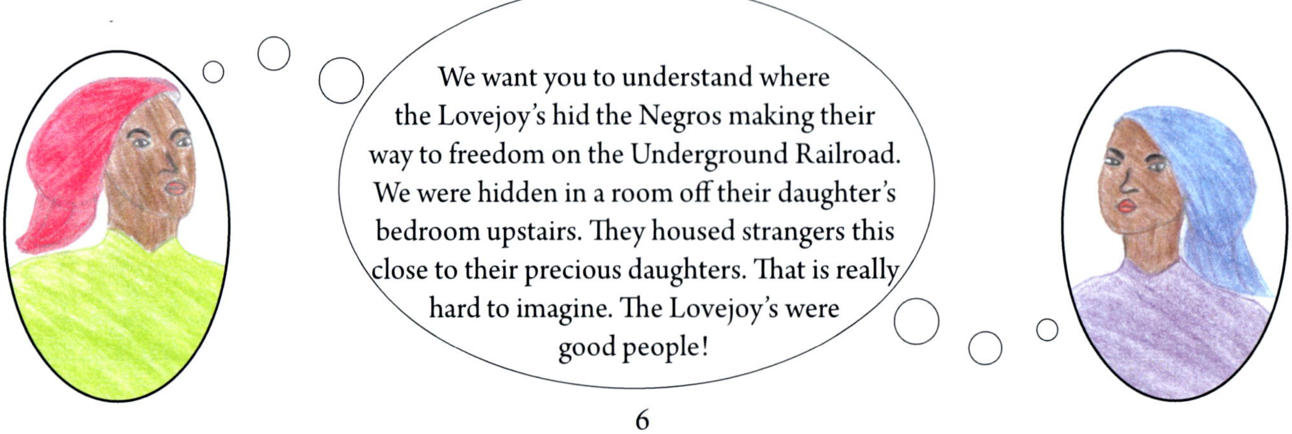

We want you to understand where the Lovejoy's hid the Negros making their way to freedom on the Underground Railroad. We were hidden in a room off their daughter's bedroom upstairs. They housed strangers this close to their precious daughters. That is really hard to imagine. The Lovejoy's were good people!

The Judge agreed with Owen, and he was immediately found not guilty and let go. Owen went home and continued helping every person, including slaves, who came to his door and needed help.

If he would have been convicted of harboring slaves, Owen would have gone to jail leaving his wife and children to take care of themselves. When he was let go, he went right back to helping runaway slaves get to freedom in the north. Very few people are brave enough to do the right thing no matter what. Are you this brave?

In 1854, Owen was elected to the Illinois House of Representatives. While there, Owen helped to organize the new Republican Party, to which Abraham Lincoln also belonged. Owen fought to end slavery in the United States, and was elected to the U.S. Congress in 1856. He served there until his death in 1864. He fought very hard for abolition, and Owen was one of a small group of people who were present for the first reading of the Emancipation Proclamation of 1863.

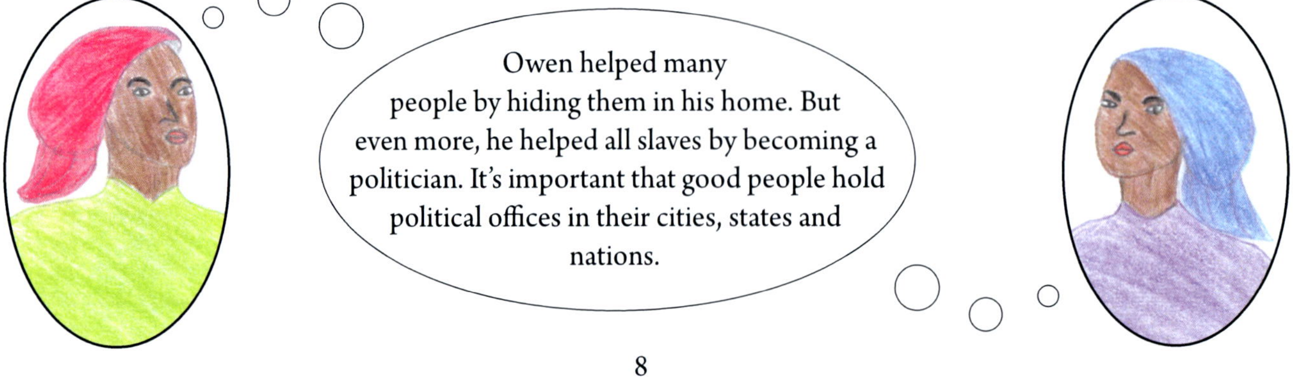

Owen helped many people by hiding them in his home. But even more, he helped all slaves by becoming a politician. It's important that good people hold political offices in their cities, states and nations.

When the Civil War broke out, Owen felt called to duty by his country. He joined the infantry as a Colonel under General Fremont. He went around to hospitals of the wounded and prayed with them. He talked with them to help raise their spirits. Aside from his chaplain role, he also served as a judge in compensation cases for the people of Missouri. When a farmer's land or livestock was taken, Owen would decide how much money they would be paid in return. While serving the Union, Owen took a leave of absence from his work in Congress. He returned to Congress a few years later, and continued his duties as a Congressman until he died.

War is very difficult. Owen visited the wounded and prayed with them. He gave comfort to those who were frightened, which is a very important job.

Owen died on March 25, 1864. While he did not live to see the end of the Civil War, he did live to see the end of slavery. Owen is buried in Princeton, in the old section of Oakland Cemetery, along with his family. Owen's son, Elijah, was left in charge of the family farm, and Owen's beloved wife, Eunice, stayed in their home until her death at age eighty-nine. Owen is remembered as a man who would do what was right because it was right, and he always helped anyone who came looking for help. After his death, Abraham Lincoln remembered him by saying, "To the day of his death, it would scarcely wrong any other to say, he was my most generous friend."

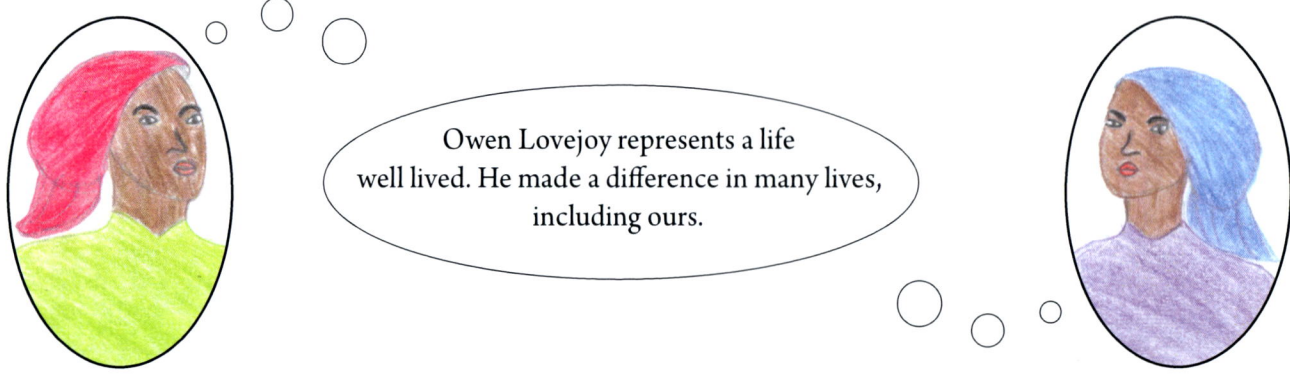

10

From the Family Album

Owen Lovejoy

Original Lovejoy Homestead

Eunice Lovejoy

In August of 2013, students affiliated with the Martin Luther King Center in Rock Island, Illinois, along with high school exchange students attending various high schools in the Quad Cities area, toured the Lovejoy Homestead. It was the largest group of African Americans to ever take a tour at one time. In addition, Deb Bowen's foreign students from Kenya, South Africa, Morocco, Tanzania, Kuwait, Azerbaijan, Bahrain, Turkey, Egypt, India, Serbia and the Philippines were excited to learn about the Underground Railroad. This tour was set up by author Kate Morrow before she went away to college.

Owen Lovejoy
"Conductor" of Underground Railroad
January 6, 1811 - March 25, 1864

"The time is always right to do what is right."
-Dr. Martin Luther King Jr.

The Underground Railroad was maintained in the northern states to aid runaway slaves in their attempt to reach freedom in Canada. It wasn't a real railroad and it was not under the ground. It was called "underground" because it was a secret and "railroad" because it seemed to run regularly like a train route.

Princeton was possibly the most important "station" in Illinois because of Reverend Owen Lovejoy. He was born in Albion, Maine and moved to Alton, Illinois as a young adult. There he studied for the ministry while living with his older brother, Elijah, who was the editor of an abolitionist newspaper. After Elijah was murdered in November of 1837 by pro-slavery forces, Owen vowed to carry on his work to end slavery.

Lovejoy accepted a position in Princeton as minister of the Hampshire Colony Congregational Church and moved there in 1838. He rented a room from Butler and Eunice Denham and, when Mr. Denham died in 1841, Lovejoy married his widow two years later. The couple had six children of their own in addition to the three daughters from Mrs. Lovejoy's first marriage. The farm became known as the Lovejoy Homestead, even though Lovejoy never owned any of the property.

It is believed that Butler and Eunice Denham hid fugitive slaves in their home before Owen Lovejoy lived there, but certainly, after Lovejoy became head of the household, the Underground Railroad was very active. In 1843 he was indicted by the grand jury for harboring two slave women; but was acquitted at his trial.

He used the pulpit to speak out against slavery and, also, became involved in the Underground Railroad. Later, he entered national politics as a way to continue his crusade against slavery. He was elected to Congress in 1856 and served there until his death in 1864.

Lovejoy was a platform speaker in support of Abraham Lincoln in his famous debates with Stephen Douglas. While in Congress, he introduced the final bill to end slavery in the District of Columbia. This was a goal of the American Anti-Slavery Society. He also helped gain passage of legislation prohibiting slavery in the territories. He was one of the few steadfast Congressional supporters of Lincoln during the American Civil War. Lincoln wrote, *"To the day of his death, it would scarcely wrong any other to say, he was my most generous friend."*

Princeton was on the Quincy route of the Underground Railroad in Illinois. Runaway slaves came up the Mississippi River and stopped at many stations between Quincy and Galesburg before reaching Princeton. Each stop was usually about ten miles apart. From Princeton, the slaves would have traveled on to one of several towns that harbored fugitives, including LaMoille, Paw Paw, LaSalle-Peru, Ottawa and Somonauk. The choice often depended on which town was the safest at that particular time. At other times, Underground Railroad operators would transport a runaway slave to a nearby village.

The trip to Canada could possibly take a year. The best time to run was during holidays or on a weekend. In that way time often went by before someone noticed the slave was gone. The hardest part of running away was knowing one may never see family or friends again. The slaves learned basic methods to keep running the right direction. Transportation was sometimes by wagon with the slave hidden under a load of hay or straw, but many walked during the night when the North Star could guide them to safety. During the day, remembering that moss grows on the north side of trees was valuable. Wading in streams confused dogs that were tracking runaway slaves. The travelers had much to remember, and fear was their constant companion.

Members of The Underground Railroad often used specific terms, based on the metaphor of the railway. For example:

· People who helped slaves find the railroad were "agents" (or "shepherds").
· Guides were known as "conductors."
· Free or escaped blacks (sometimes whites) who helped guide fugitives were "abductors."
· Hiding places were "stations."
· "Station masters" hid slaves in their homes.
· Escaped slaves were referred to as "passengers" or "cargo."
· Slaves would obtain a "ticket."
· Financial benefactors of the Railroad were known as "stockholders."

Elijah Lovejoy (November 9, 1802 - November 7, 1837)

Elijah Lovejoy was a Presbyterian minister, journalist, newspaper editor and abolitionist. He was murdered by a pro-slavery mob in Alton, Illinois, during an attack to destroy his printing press and abolitionist materials.

"Slavery must cease to exist. There can be no doubt on this subject."

-Elijah P. Lovejoy

""I have decided to stick with love. Hate is too great a burden to bear."
-Dr. Martin Luther King Jr.

About the Author
Kate Morrow

Kate's loving and history-obsessed family and their cats moved to Princeton when she was in the fourth grade. During high school, she was involved in many activities including pom squad, tennis and Student Council. Her first visit to the Lovejoy Homestead was on a school field trip and she remembers seeing the Agnes and Nancy figures peeking out of their hideaway. She learned how to differentiate the facts from the fiction of the commonly told story of escaping slaves. This inspired her to spend her senior summer working as a tour guide at the Lovejoy home on weekends. She enjoyed the opportunity to deepen her knowledge and explore all things mid-nineteenth century!

Morrow was given the task of weaving together the story covering slavery and politics during the 1860s, Lincoln's presidency, Owen and Elijah Lovejoy's lives, and daily life in and around the house during those years. Through this process, Kate felt like she came to know and understand Owen as a real person. After meeting Deb Bowen and giving her a tour, she was thrilled to be asked to bring a 150-year-old tale back to life for young readers. She hopes this story inspires them to learn and enjoy history as vibrant and alive rather than dusty and forgotten.

About the Illustrator
Rashida Juma

Rashida Juma from Kenya as an exchange student with the Kennedy-Lugar Youth Exchange and Study (YES) program for the 2013-2014 school year. She attended Mercer County High School in Aledo, Illinois and successfully completed her academic year in America. She was excited to participate on the girl's basketball team and also enjoyed a wide variety of community service activities. She was hosted by the Milburn family who will miss Rashida and her beautiful smile.

If you are interested in hosting an inbound exchange student or going outbound, contact dbowenexchange@gmail.com or your local Rotary club.

A BOOK by ME®
OPERATION WRITE NOW

"I'm asking ordinary children to do something extraordinary!"

Deb Bowen, Creator & Director
www.abookbyme.com

I'm asking ordinary children all over the world to use their talents to share extraordinary stories. Many students write about Holocaust survivors, Righteous Gentiles (non-Jews who risked their lives to save the Jewish people), prison camp liberators and other important stories of World War II. Since this generation is getting older, the time to interview them, write and illustrate their important story is RIGHT NOW!

Some students are deciding to tell important stories about human rights or heroes as well. Check out the website and then decide what interests you. The writer's guidelines are online, and you can register your story once you decide who your subject will be. Also, online you will find a sample of a newspaper article you could use to find a subject in your hometown. Talking to a grandparent, visiting nursing homes, VFW or meeting with a local historian might lead you to a possible story.

All authors / illustrators must be age 18 or under to qualify. All submissions will be given consideration for the A BOOK by ME® series, but there is no guarantee the work will be published.

It is my hope you have learned from the book you just read and are interested in reading more work by young authors. It would delight me to know you are inspired to write a book about a subject important to you.

Be careful and watch yourselves closely so you do not forget the things your eyes have seen or let them slip from your heart as long as you live. Teach them to your children and to your children's children.
Deuteronomy 4:9

CYA Calling Youth to Action

1 Kouski's Kids

The War and the Boy shares the remarkable experiences of Roy Kouski, an American soldier in Europe during World War II. Roy's moving story was written by his granddaughter, Brittany Ern. CYA challenges young people who love writing or art to take part in a book project through A BOOK by ME. Make Roy and Brittany proud by becoming one of Kouski's Kids! Check out the writer's guidelines at www.abookbyme.com.

2 Mwalimu's Dream

Mwalimu, a young man from Kenya, came to the USA as a foreign exchange student and went home a young author through A BOOK by ME. Read Mwalimu's Dream to learn how he changed thousands of lives in his village with the gift of clean water. There are still many villages that need wells. CYA hopes your classroom is moved to contribute spare change to dig water wells in undeveloped countries. Your small change can make a big change in someone's life! Take a look at www.wells4wellness.com.

3 Change the World

After World War II, student exchange was created to encourage foreign youth to study in the United States. Exchange provides opportunities to build relationships and share cultures which creates better understanding and mutual respect. People whose countries have been former enemies have become "family" through exchange. Hosts are responsible to provide room and board, love and support. The student provides his/her own spending money and health insurance. Host families are always needed. Contact dbowenexchange@gmail.com to learn more.

LEARNING STATION

Vocabulary and Key Terms

abolitionist – a person who advocated and supported the end of slavery in the U.S. prior to the Civil War

Abraham Lincoln – the 16th president of the U.S., who led the fight for saving the Union in the Civil War and for the emancipation of slaves

civil rights – legal claims that protect individuals' freedom, including the ensuring of peoples' physical and mental integrity, life and safety, protection from discrimination on grounds of race, gender, sexual orientation, gender identity, national origin, color, ethnicity, religion, or disability

Civil War – a war in the U.S. from 1861 to 1865 between the North and South states over political and economic issues including the issue of slavery

Congress – the national legislative body of the U.S. with responsibilities of lawmaking, instituting taxes, regulating commerce, supporting military, approving presidential appointments, etc

Emancipation Proclamation – a declaration issued by President Lincoln on January 1, 1863, freeing the slaves under the Confederacy

printing press – a machine for printing on paper

slavery – ownership of a person as personal property; forcing a person into work without pay

Underground Railroad – a system of aiding escaped southern slaves who moved usually at night to "stations," secret houses and other places as they made their way north to freedom

Short Summary

During times of slavery, Owen Lovejoy lived in the free state of Illinois. After his brother was murdered for his work in the abolition movement, Owen became more passionate about ending slavery. He studied to become a pastor and worked in Princeton, Illinois, where he hid runaway slaves in his own home as a "station" on the Underground Railroad.

MLA Citation

Morrow, Kate. *Living with Lovejoy.* Vol. 14. Ill. Juma, Rashida Mohamed. Aledo: Never Forget, 2015. Print. Human Rights Ser.

Topics Covered

Anti-Bullying
Black History
Compassion
Perseverance
Slavery

LEARNING STATION

Thinking Strategies

- Making Connections – Connect the reading to the existing schema.
- Questioning – Question before, during, and after reading. Consider the content, ideas, and events.
- Visualizing – Use background knowledge, make mental pictures of the text.
- Inferring – Use knowledge to infer the underlying theme or idea to interpret meaning.
- Determining Importance – Develop summarizing skills.
- Synthesizing – Make sense of important information to construct deeper meaning.

Pre-Reading Activity

Read this excerpt from *The Underground Railroad in Western Illinois* by Owen W. Muelder:

> By early November of that year [Elijah] Lovejoy had witnessed the destruction of his printing presses on three different occasions by proslavery forces. When a fourth press arrived November 6th, he and his loyal supporters stood guard to protect it from those who might again try to take it from him. The next night a drunken mob formed and the scene soon turned ugly. The abolitionist-hating rioters charged the building where Lovejoy and his friends were waiting, shots rang out, and one man in the crowd outside was killed. The mob retreated, reorganized, and the town went into a frenzy. The anti-abolitionist horde then charged the building for a second time and set it on fire. When Lovejoy emerged to examine the extent of the flames, he was felled by bullets and died.

How do you think the death of Owen Lovejoy's brother, Elijah, might have impacted him?

Related Literature & Media

A BOOK by ME Human Rights Series*
- Book #2 *Governor Coles – The Second Governor of Illinois* is about the election of Governor Coles and his ideal of keeping Illinois a state free.
- Book #3 *The Boy in the Glass Coffin* is the story of Emmett Till, the African-American boy who was murdered in Mississippi.
- Book #4 *Rosa Parks: A Woman in Power* is about a worldwide legend who is known for her courage to defy bigotry in the south.

Other Books*
- *His Brother's Blood: Speeches and Writings, 1838-64* by Owen Lovejoy is a collection of speeches and writings by Owen Lovejoy.
- *The Underground Railroad in Western Illinois* by Owen W. Muelder tells many true stories of the Underground Railroad in Illinois.

*Preview all literature for appropriateness for the age group

Technology

Have students write mini-book reports to post on the A BOOK by ME Facebook page where others will read about their opinion of ABBM stories. Review with students how to write descriptions and to summarize. Include the theme and lessons learned. Remind students to be respectful in their writings. All posts on the Facebook page will be monitored.

 facebook.com / A BOOK by ME

LEARNING STATION

Discussion Questions

1) What is an abolitionist? What goals might an abolitionist have? Why do you think Owen dedicated his life to helping the cause of abolishing slavery? What did he sacrifice to pursue his dream of ending slavery?

2) Owen chose not to work at an Episcopal Church because he wouldn't be allowed to preach abolition in the church. Why was it so important for Owen? What ideals do you have that you wouldn't sacrifice for a job?

3) Owen met Abraham Lincoln when he was elected to the Illinois House of Representatives. Afterwards, he got involved with the campaign to help Lincoln win the presidential election. Why did he get along so well with Lincoln? What did Lincoln say about Owen after he died?

Extended Activities

A) The Lovejoy Homestead is where Owen raised his family and helped slaves escape on the Underground Railroad. The home is now open for tours. Access www.lovejoyhomestead.com to learn more about Owen, his family, the Underground Railroad, and life back in 1840's and 50's.

B) In a speech in Greenup, Illinois, Owen told this story about a slave he encountered.
"On a plantation, in the distant Southland, in the low miasmatic swamps, there was a woman. She was young, handsome, and under God's law had as much right to live and control her own actions as any of us. She was of one-eighth African blood, just like your blood and mine. The overseer of the plantation where she was held in bondage sought to persecute her because she would not assent to his advances. She escaped into the swamps. Bloodhounds were set on her trail. She boarded a little steamboat which plied on a small river which emptied into the great Father of waters. In the fullness of time she landed at the first station in Illinois, name not given, and proceeded from station to station. Finally she arrived in Princeton. I myself was the keeper of that station at Princeton. She came to my house hungry and told me her story. She was fairer than my own daughter, proud, tall and beautiful. She was naked and I clothed her; she was hungry and I gave her bread; she was penniless and I gave her money. She was unable to reach the next station and I sent her to it. So from station to station she crossed the Northland far from baying dogs on her trail, and out from under the shadow of the flag we love and venerate, into Canada. Today she lives there a free and happy woman."

Owen describes the woman well. Illustrate what you think she might have looked like. Incorporate in the drawing one word to describe her. Display the illustration as a reminder of Owen's story and his ideals.

C) The posters to the right were used to persuade people to return runaway slaves. Create a poster to hang up in your school that encourages others to be a generous friend.

LEARNING STATION

Bullying Definition

According to Olweus Bullying Prevention Program: "A person is bullied when he or she is exposed, repeatedly and over time, to negative actions on the part of one or more other persons, and he or she has difficulty defending himself or herself."

Discussion Questions Relating to Bullying

Do you see examples of bullying in *Living with Lovejoy*?
How does this story compare to bullying situations in your own school or community?
What can you do to stop bullying from taking place?

Anti-Bullying Role Playing

Role playing is a way for students to internalize different responses and practices to reduce conflict in social situations. Review the possible coping strategies with students. Discuss how to deal with a specific bullying situation. Once the group decides on an appropriate coping strategy(s), students can act it out. Take note that the bully could react in a variety of different ways.

4 ways to describe emotion:

- crushed
- discarded
- hated
- unchosen

Situation: A young boy is treated badly by his peers because of his skin color. People call him names and don't include him in social settings. What could the boy do to address this bullying? What could others do to help him?

Bullying Coping Strategies

- **Avoidance** – Find a way to ignore the bully. Sometimes attention is what the bully wants.
- **Assertiveness** – Sometimes the best way to deal with a bully is to defend yourself by telling them to leave you alone. If you are watching someone else being bullied, stand up for that person.
- **Friendship** – Strength in numbers will sometimes put a bully in his/her place. Find someone who will stand up with you. Be the person who defends a victim of a bully.
- **Education** – Find an adult (teacher, parent, mentor, etc.) to help you educate others about treating all people with respect. If a bully won't back down, get someone with authority to help you stop the situation.

Advice from Owen's Story

Be a generous friend.
Have students discuss and/or write how this advice could be used in their life.

LEARNING STATION

Comprehension Questions
Cite evidence from the story text in your answers.

1. Owen Lovejoy was an abolitionist. What does that mean? _____
_____
_____
_____

2. Describe Owen's life in Princeton in 1838. _____
_____
_____
_____

3. What was the Underground Railroad? _____
_____
_____
_____

4. How did Owen prove his innocence in court when he was accused of helping two slaves? _____
_____
_____
_____

5. What was Owen's job when he served in the Civil War? _____

6. What was the Emancipation Proclamation? _____
_____
_____
_____

7. What did Abraham Lincoln say about Owen? _____
_____
_____

8. What did you learn from Owen's story? _____
_____
_____
_____

LEARNING STATION

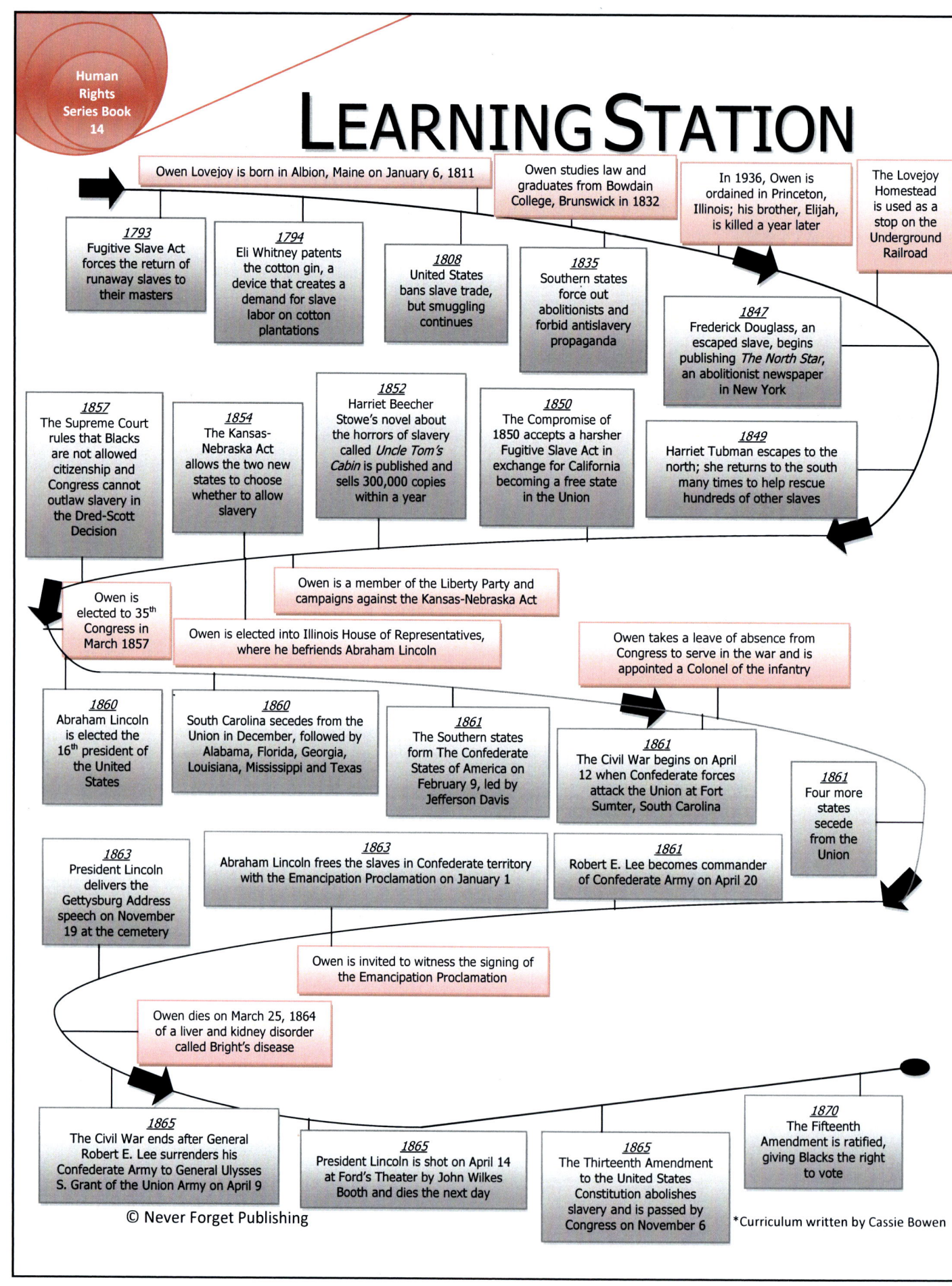

Owen Lovejoy is born in Albion, Maine on January 6, 1811

Owen studies law and graduates from Bowdain College, Brunswick in 1832

In 1936, Owen is ordained in Princeton, Illinois; his brother, Elijah, is killed a year later

The Lovejoy Homestead is used as a stop on the Underground Railroad

1793
Fugitive Slave Act forces the return of runaway slaves to their masters

1794
Eli Whitney patents the cotton gin, a device that creates a demand for slave labor on cotton plantations

1808
United States bans slave trade, but smuggling continues

1835
Southern states force out abolitionists and forbid antislavery propaganda

1847
Frederick Douglass, an escaped slave, begins publishing *The North Star*, an abolitionist newspaper in New York

1857
The Supreme Court rules that Blacks are not allowed citizenship and Congress cannot outlaw slavery in the Dred-Scott Decision

1854
The Kansas-Nebraska Act allows the two new states to choose whether to allow slavery

1852
Harriet Beecher Stowe's novel about the horrors of slavery called *Uncle Tom's Cabin* is published and sells 300,000 copies within a year

1850
The Compromise of 1850 accepts a harsher Fugitive Slave Act in exchange for California becoming a free state in the Union

1849
Harriet Tubman escapes to the north; she returns to the south many times to help rescue hundreds of other slaves

Owen is a member of the Liberty Party and campaigns against the Kansas-Nebraska Act

Owen is elected to 35th Congress in March 1857

Owen is elected into Illinois House of Representatives, where he befriends Abraham Lincoln

Owen takes a leave of absence from Congress to serve in the war and is appointed a Colonel of the infantry

1860
Abraham Lincoln is elected the 16th president of the United States

1860
South Carolina secedes from the Union in December, followed by Alabama, Florida, Georgia, Louisiana, Mississippi and Texas

1861
The Southern states form The Confederate States of America on February 9, led by Jefferson Davis

1861
The Civil War begins on April 12 when Confederate forces attack the Union at Fort Sumter, South Carolina

1861
Four more states secede from the Union

1863
President Lincoln delivers the Gettysburg Address speech on November 19 at the cemetery

1863
Abraham Lincoln frees the slaves in Confederate territory with the Emancipation Proclamation on January 1

1861
Robert E. Lee becomes commander of Confederate Army on April 20

Owen is invited to witness the signing of the Emancipation Proclamation

Owen dies on March 25, 1864 of a liver and kidney disorder called Bright's disease

1865
The Civil War ends after General Robert E. Lee surrenders his Confederate Army to General Ulysses S. Grant of the Union Army on April 9

1865
President Lincoln is shot on April 14 at Ford's Theater by John Wilkes Booth and dies the next day

1865
The Thirteenth Amendment to the United States Constitution abolishes slavery and is passed by Congress on November 6

1870
The Fifteenth Amendment is ratified, giving Blacks the right to vote

*Curriculum written by Cassie Bowen